QUICKER THAN THE EYE

Quicker Than the Eye

JOE FIORITO

THE POETRY IMPRINT AT VÉHICULE PRESS

Published with the generous assistance of the Canada Council for the Arts and the Canada Book Fund of the Department of Canadian Heritage.

SIGNAL EDITIONS EDITOR: CARMINE STARNINO

Cover design by David Drummond
Photo of the author by Richard Lautens
Set in Minion and Filosofia by Simon Garamond
Printed by Marquis Book Printing Inc.

Dépôt légal, Library and Archives Canada and the Bibliothèque national du Québec, third trimester 2023

Published by Véhicule Press, Montréal, Québec, Canada
www.vehiculepress.com

Distribution in Canada by LitDistCo
www.litdistco.ca

Distributed in the US by Independent Publishers Group
www.ipgbook.com

Printed in Canada on FSC certified paper.

CONTENTS

THREE

I, too, dislike it.

—MARIANNE MOORE, "Poetry"

INTRODUCTION

In an instant, there is a person, a thing, an action.

One sees what happens, and how, and the instant is an instant memory.

The memory becomes a story, but when it is told it becomes not the original story but the story as it was heard by the one who listened, and those two things are rarely the same.

As you see, this is a tricky business.

Such caution informed my work as a journalist; getting the instant wrong was a terror. I am still a journalist of sorts, but now there is both joy and anticipation; poetry
is quicker than the eye.

One

Vaccination

I was stabbed
with a pin-sharp
pencil,

HB, Grade 3,
my right shoulder,
by a friend.

He mimed a kill;
the lead broke off
in me.

I have the scar
and use a pencil
still.

After Borges

As I grow old
and less like myself—
or like I never

was—what I recall
is not the thing,
but a memory

of the thing:
her lips, a memory
of her lips,

the memory of
a memory of
her lips.

After Monet

four figures
harm a landscape.
I am a tree.

sur l'herbe is
a rough ménage:
three clothed,

one nude.
I loathe her
and me.

How The Carver Got His Stitches

I asked him if he'd ever cut,
as butchers do, his hand.
(every scar, a story.)

No; not until the next day
in distracted thought.
(my fault, sorry.)

Annex Billiards

for John Ferri

green baize is
my weekly vice;

then to Kenzo:
shoyu ramen,

gyoza, lemon
soda, ice.

A Great Confusion

I am heading north
although it feels as if I am
heading south

but I am coming from
the south. I am
distraught.

I am trying to avoid
all those places
you are not.

The Boxer

I have gold teeth.
I have silver scissors.
I cut hair

and I fight. I was
heavy this morning,
skipped rope

and lost three lbs.
I can go six rounds
on eggs,

toast, and coffee.
I have an exhibition
at Sully's tonight.

I have all my fights
in all my thoughts
all night.

Courtroom Hallway

The x-ray shows
my skull is a web
of cracks.

My eyes are red.
I'd knelt to see if
I could get

a tractor unstuck.
The tire rolled across
my head—

lucky me, muck's
not rock, I get that,
but fuck.

ESL Fatigue

Why should I try
to know the names
of animals,

the spiny fish
of Lake Ontario,
or flowers?

Your birds and
your trees are not
ours.

Workfare Blues

in the pancake
house with my soi-disant
welfare mouse:

have any dish you wish
means bacon, runny eggs,
cakes & sausages.

I asked, do you make
a living & he said I draw
my wages &

they claw back;
how can you save when
they make you pay

for the shovel you use
to dig your own
grave?

Fred and Barb

She bathed his feet,
brought soup in a thermos
to make him fatter.

It didn't matter.

He died. She got his papers.
She died. I got his papers;
plus his thumb-worn

stacks of porn.

Scribbled on the beaver pix
in ink: amo, amas, amat –
guttural, and

meant to flatter.

Grace Ward

on her lap
green leaves & blue
flowers

a snapshot, close-up—
lithodora diffusa, a.k.a.
grace ward

in a teacup; on her
balcony, a pretty thing
to overlook.

Attenborough Boogie-Woogie

a seal's
first thought:
shake free.

a second
thought: death,
come for me.

orca's thought:
how bountiful
the sea.

What Adonidas Saw

i.m. Bruno Gerussi

shale & seashell
detritus of old boats

cedar logs, arbutus
limbs & dead-

heads in salt water;
rope & float.

Her Windowsill

lavender in a pot
and lemons in a dish

dispel the smell
of frying fish.

Corso Italia

I, with his ma, us shopping
when she stopped
to stare,

to squint & point & glare—
"Who's that sad old man
over there?"

On the patio of the Dip,
with book & cup, her son.
I shut up.

Folk Tale

a woman, a man,
a ewe, a ram

on a farm in the fall.
she said no

and he said yes.
straw is rough

and hay is warm.
in the spring

came the lamb;
here I am.

Two

Where I'm From

the desolate things
are mine: the dry dirt road,
the hull of a truck,

tar paper, ditched;
the smell of twitch grass,
red-hot rust flakes

on the rims of paint cans;
chalky sheetrock:
home.

Saint Teresa

milk tea on a tray
a spray of camellias for
her birthday—

my aunt Tree, mute post-
stroke, until my dad
began to play:

she sang please
don't take something some-
thing away.

I and My Brothers

we were four;
three of us are no more—
they, doomed

to die in rented rooms
from drugs & drink
or push & shove,

were done in
by the want—not mine
—of love.

The Baby Brother

for T. F.

He used to sleep all day.
I used to wonder why.
Now that I am older, I think
he knew he'd die.

After me in life, he was
ahead of me in many things:
music, love, rage,
cocaine,

cancer, liquor, meth.
He was ahead of me in death.
Had he lived, we'd have
talked late and long.

Now I ache. I can't sleep.
I am wary of my drugs and
uncertain of my song.
I hold my breath.

Ma's Cows

dolly, clover,
heather, belle

lowing,
full with milk

now boss, ho,
bos, ever thus:

bos taurus
typicus.

The Three-Room Farmhouse

My ma, sweet sixteen, had
to sleep on the floor in the room
with her dead pa,

although his funeral was
off-limits: she was too young,
would be undone

to see him in his coffin
in the grave; was left to grieve
alone.

Farm is big, town is small,
and news is fast: the man who
craved her

knew she'd be—knew they'd be—
(don't cry, don't tell) alone
at last.

The Family Story

I, my ma, and my half-
brother in a sleeper
to Swan River,

so bored so bored so
bored I tore the arms from
my lead Hussars

all the way to the scene
of the crime: a three-room
farmhouse, black

woodstove, lino cracked,
soft spuds with must-
white eyes

in sacks. Later in the hen-
house, he found an egg:
two yolks and

a blood spot.
I kept his secret and
refused to eat.

Kettle Rapids

for E. B.

A flat rock and other
rocks in the river.
I don't swim; she sun-
bathed.

The water was slow
and cold until we saw
him; then it was
fast.

He paused
as if he did not mean
to push me off and her
down.

I was ready to drown.
He seemed not to care.
I am here instead
of there.

The Tenth Grade Zen of the Sisters of St. Joseph

My oldest nun asked
which was the fuller vessel—
a thimble, or a cup.

Sister, I said, it all depends—
am I drinking water, or
rye and 7-Up?

A Notice Of Eviction

I don't shoot in stairwells
anymore, altho I relapse
now and then.

I am afraid of elevators
and parking lots: stabbed
here and there.

If you write my reply
sign it, "Yours truly,
pepper spray."

It's about the money.
I'm in limbo; she
can't pay.

He Never Saw It Coming

If you miss with a gun
the one you miss
will come

for you. This isn't
news. But I always had
one thing:

I could tell
who had a gun until
I couldn't.

My Beautiful Geraniums

I am steadfast,
right to deadhead
red them

daily; if I do not,
there is rot:
botrytis

spotted leaf,
spider webs,
mites.

Rose in Pieces

half of her was
here, hiding in plain
sight

half of her was
there, draped
in a sheet

dark blood where
her legs used to
meet.

She Said

they will see
a female body
with a penis

and a plastic
heart—talk about
that part

my pix, my audio
this beauty is
my art.

She Did

all her surgeries,
faced alone: skin peeled,
bone shaved,

brow and jawline
pared; after which, boys
stared.

and down there?
are you a perv, are you
a cop?

post-op, still sore,
her mother can't abide her
anymore.

She Undid

The clasp of my jacket collar
caught her angora

as we, in her doorway, cheek-
kissed. She, quick, unhooked

me from her without a look.
I can't say it wasn't

thrilling, or that I'd have been
unwilling.

The Bedbug Raiders

they came
and took my stuff
at night—

my books,
my clothes, my bed,
my art.

I can't take
my cat in her cage
because

they took my cart.
I'll see red until
I'm dead.

The Jewelled Stair's Complaint

I seal my door
at night, the smell is
an attack.

Her nightie is dirty
front and back.
Her gums

are bloody, her teeth
black. I ask for help;
none comes.

My Little Addict

I found her on the porch,
took my paper, let her sleep,
drank my coffee

in the kitchen; torn tee,
chill air, my wicker chair.
I guessed crack.

In the news?
her feet were slim and bare.
I draped her

in a quilt and felt a creep.
I never saw her go. I knew
she'd be back.

Poem in the Manner of Her Poems

She spoke of the library
and what she did there—
of the hospital

and what was done to her
there—of her first kiss
with that boy, Bob.

Bob, a boy no more,
lives half a block from me;
we've never kissed.

The library is not far
away. I have no card, so
nothing due.

I saw a woman die
in that hospital; as near
to me as you.

100 Park Bench Plaza

on a white paper sheet
her hand-lined grid
scored ten

by ten, each square
numbered; she stabs
her fore-

finger again, aloud,
again: nine-seven,
nine-eight,

nine-nine; no
more.

Adanac Hotel

his blood is
a red spit-whip,
slo-mo

in air. I kicked
him there—
no one here

says that to me,
I'll kick them
anywhere.

The Arthur Street Affair

The door lets in
slashes of kicked light:
her place, midnight

& me, naked
in his chair; he knows
I'm there.

She tells him to go
away. He is so drunk
he obeys.

A minute more:
her floor, my blood
galore.

Hot Love

a dead dog
on a broken knee—
your love for me.

a swollen cheek,
the bruises new—
my love for you.

Breakup Note

I do not see you
anymore and
here's

the reason why:
you cut me and
I cut you—

your hand is
quicker than
my eye.

Three

Of a Hatchling on the Sidewalk in the Winter

Tucking the featherless thing
into a lost glove—her hands warm,
her breath hot—

she told us, as we stopped to look,
that it was okay at first but
now it's not.

Rom Com

Daddy knows your flame
is a mondegreen—her hot song
in yellow tights

against the trailing descant
of his singalong: women want
it just as much as men.

Not now, not then.

She walks to The Bay.
He glides down the railing
into Museum Station.

In translation?

She wanted to be held.
He'd have held her;
not today.

Streetcar Serenade

Hello, baby doll.
Do you take yours double-
double?

(I take it black.)

I was in jail with women
in New York. I just got back.
I was married

to a jerk—

he wouldn't work.
Are you married? Do you
love cartoons?

(I looked at my shoe.)

I like Fred and Barney,
Betty, Wilma, Bam-Bam,
Hopparoo.

(Me, too.)

The Oldest Man In Shelter

He missed the war
and had a car: did he have
a lot of girls?

His flickering eye,
his yellow hair, his spit-
combed curls,

his arm tattoo, a blue
swallow with a trailing
ribbon

unfurling "happiness"
on inky veins; his wet cough.
Don Juan in thin

pin-striped pajamas:
"I picked up where you
left off."

Men and Kisses

Jack paid for his
with his cap, which
I kept.

Doc traced his
fortune on my palm.
I was calm.

Yves would've
had me and his wife
in their bed.

I was a woman:
headache,
I said.

His Left Hand

I was shot in the belly.
My legs turned to jelly.
I dropped, got up—
pop-pop, pop

again, dropped again.
My guts are scarred, my jaw
is clenched,

my hand is a claw.
I can't pull a trigger
I'm not going to
carry.

Short Takes

1
His key, her lock, flick
of light, drip of tap.
"Honey, stay."

2
His money, her purse.
A liar is not a friend.
A thief is worse.

3
Her swollen arm.
She washed, with gas,
the smell of him away.

Lockdown, Month Six

I see your lists
of movies, hot tunes,
cat pix,

selfies, puns,
loaves of bread,
uncut hair,

garden views,
birthday news:
don't care.

Lip Gloss

All you all gonna get
some slaps—

at her age I didn't
know very much very

well. Sparkly nails
tug at bra straps,

all old men end up
in hell.

Fred Dunn's 80th Birthday

A cake will catch fire.
I gave five puffs and have nothing
to prove but

my love. Nurse Barb claps hands.
I am true to myself, I am
Polonius in a tent,

or I am his son. I have the habit
of telling the truth; truth is,
I don't like cake.

Adam in Eden

My basil was better
last year; it should be higher—
too hot, too dry.

My apple tree always
had flowers; this year,
sigh.

My garden starts, stops—
until this year I had not seen
tomatoes die.

Deaf Blind Haircut

In my hand, the hair
of the blind man
in my chair.

Warm air whispers
in his ear; he cannot
hear.

He feels the scissors
and the clipper's heat.
Cut neat,

he cannot hear;
warm air whispers
in his ear.

Local Citrus Seller Tells All

Some guys buy oranges
better. Here, it's dog eat dog
or dog eat rat.

My pineapples are
twenty on the ten. The cash
in my wallet

pays my bills. He is hung over
and has Buddha's hands
on pallets.

Late Night Korean Snack Store

The Pepero Original
is chocolate, the Nude
is not.

I love Pocky, Hello Panda,
Hello Choco Home-
Run Ball.

Try the Jerky Squid,
Roasted Squid, Butter
Squid, all squids.

I'd eat Halo
Seaweed Chili Lime
all the time

if I could, you should, it is
nothing less than
very good.

Front Row

jeté,
pirouette

from her
to me

a single drop
of sweat

After The Move

I am learning how
to die in this part of town—
when in Rome, etc.

New to me, the streetcar
stop, the curb cut. I stumble
and fall;

this is my proof of payment
all the way, all the way
home.

The Oratory of St. Joseph

One crutch does not
stink but heaps of crutches
do—the salt smell

of stuttered prayers,
ex voto hearts, tin hands,
tin feet,

tin eyes. all the dull
miracles pinned in rows
along a wall.

When the tree fell on
St. Joseph's pup, he saw
stars;

now he sees me,
knees bent, trying not
to fall.

Ibiza, 1968

The butcher mixed
chorizo in a bucket
in the alley

slapping at the flies
on his red arms, his face,
his apron.

I held her hand
in mine; his bloody
grin

when the one
who held the camera
snapped.

Steelhead, Mackenzie

spring creek, ice
black, sun in
my eyes—

the spasm
of a trout between
my thighs

One Last Fishing Trip

for Ken Conrad

We drove your old man to the lake;
heavy on the gas, light on the brake.

The water was cold, oily-thick.
The rocks on shore, mossy and slick.

I saw you watch each cast
as if it were his last.

October, North Shore

nothing hides
as the last heat
declines

blue water, blue
granite, and ravens
in white pines

The Day He Died

for Al Jack

She scratched
the win for life.
He, over there,

said "Hey, Pussy,
got a light?"

She looked up
because pussy is
a word.

Pussy had a Bic.
She smiled.

I hear my friend
is dead. No one
wins for life.

A Souvenir Coin

the face in
my pocket, worn
smooth

as I walk,
is a talisman
of regret.

The street kid:
"Any change?"
I observe

the obverse:
"No, not
yet."

Opal

the ring on the table
is not a ring,

it is the ring on the table,
just as the table is not

a table, it is the table
with the ring.

this is how two things
are one thing—

her table, his ring;
one thing, nothing.

NOTES ON THE POEMS

"…there is in
it after all, a place for the genuine."

–Marianne Moore, "Poetry"

The milk cow, I think it was Clover, saved my mother's life when she was a girl; she'd lost her way in a winter white-out and the sound of the cowbell led her back to the warmth of the barn. She gave me the cowbell. I was an adult when she told me the story of the rape, and her subsequent exile, and the birth of my brother.

I met E.B. in a bush camp in Gillam, Manitoba, during the construction of the Kettle Rapids Dam. We lived in Spain together for a time. I was callow. She is a painter of giant industrial landscapes.

St. Joseph's Oratory was the life-long project of Brother André, who referred to himself as St. Joseph's pup, a Catholic humble-brag if there ever was one.

I knew Rosemary Catacalos in Ibiza. We were kids then, we were learning how to write, and we were lifelong friends. She was the poet laureate of Texas. She lost her breath in 2022.

The woman in the three "She" poems is a drag mother; she has taught scores of trans men how to dress, how to do hair and makeup, how to comport themselves. Her beauty is beside the point. Oh, that's not true. She intends her body to be plasticized when she dies.

Finally, Al Jack taught high school English. He let us teach ourselves, using the standard curriculum, during the last half of Grade 13. I owe him this and all my other books.

ACKNOWLEDGEMENTS

Thank you, Carmine Starnino.

I also owe a continuing debt to all my newspaper colleagues; you can't fool them. My pals in Montreal are the dukes of badinage. The gang at Annex Billiards are more important to me than they know.

Ferri and Contenta are my brothers. Slinger and Enright endure my bad puns with good grace and volley them back with verve.

Finally, in the morning, when Susan Mahoney plays Dr. Gradus Ad Parnassum on the piano, I am as close to heaven as I will ever get.

Talya Rubin • Richard Sanger • Stephen Scobie
Peter Dale Scott • Deena Kara Shaffer
Carmine Starnino • Andrew Steinmetz • David Solway
Ricardo Sternberg • Shannon Stewart
Philip Stratford, trans. • Matthew Sweeney
Harry Thurston • Rhea Tregebov • Peter Van Toorn
Patrick Warner • Derek Webster • Anne Wilkinson
Donald Winkler, trans. • Shoshanna Wingate
Christopher Wiseman • Catriona Wright
Terence Young